BRIGHT
IDEA
BOOKS

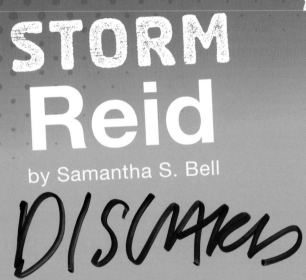

STORM
Reid

by Samantha S. Bell

DISCARD

CAPSTONE PRESS
a capstone imprint

Bright Idea Books are published by Capstone Press
1710 Roe Crest Drive, North Mankato, Minnesota 56003
www.mycapstone.com

Library of Congress Cataloging-in-Publication Data
Library of Congress Cataloging-in-Publication Data is available on the Library of Congress website.
ISBN: 978-1-5435-5790-9 (library hardcover)
978-1-5435-6035-0 (paperback)
978-1-5435-5822-7 (eBook PDF)

Editorial Credits
Editor: Claire Vanden Branden
Designer: Becky Daum
Production Specialist: Colleen McLaren

Photo Credits
Alamy: Sony Pictures/Entertainment Pictures, 20–21; AP Images: cover; Rex Features: Atsushi Nishijima/Disney/Kobal, 6–7, 24, Chelsea Lauren, 17, 27, James Gourley, 8, Jim Smeal/BEI, 12; Shutterstock Images: AJP, 30–31, Dfree, 5, f11photo, 11, Featureflash Photo Agency, 23, Kathy Hutchins, 15, Mark Dumbleton, 18–19

Printed in the United States of America.
PA48

TABLE OF CONTENTS

CHAPTER ONE
STAR TEENAGER 4

CHAPTER TWO
A YOUNG START............. 10

CHAPTER THREE
UP FOR A CHALLENGE....... 16

CHAPTER FOUR
FUTURE PLANS............... 22

Glossary 28
Timeline........................... 29
Activity 30
Further Resources............... 32
Index............................... 32

CHAPTER 1

STAR
Teenager

"Action!" said the **director**. Storm Reid walked into the room. She said her lines just as she had practiced. The director shouted, "Cut!"

Reid is like other teenagers. She hangs out with friends. She loves reading and playing with her dogs. She goes to movies with her family. She also has a job. But Reid's job is uncommon for a teenager. She is a movie star.

Storm Reid attends special events as part of her job.

Reid had the lead role in the movie *A Wrinkle in Time*. She played the main character, Meg Murry. Meg struggles in school. She feels like an **outcast**. Her father is missing. Meg must travel through time and space to find him.

A Wrinkle in Time made more than $98 million in theaters.

Reid with her director and costars from *A Wrinkle in Time*

Reid enjoyed playing the part of Meg. She learned a lot. Reid knows she is not perfect. She will make mistakes. But Meg taught Reid how to be herself. She learned to love who she is. Reid wants other girls to know that too.

A RELATABLE CAST

Many races are represented in *A Wrinkle in Time*. The director wanted all young people to **relate** to the film.

CHAPTER 2

A YOUNG Start

Reid was born on July 1, 2003. She wanted to act since she was 3 years old. Her first job was in a commercial.

Reid works hard. She wants to be good at her job. She knows it takes a lot of training. She takes acting classes. She studies **martial arts** and dance.

Reid grew up in Atlanta, Georgia.

Reid had just three small roles before *12 Years a Slave*.

STARTING OUT

Reid's first big movie part was in 2013. She was 9 years old. The movie was *12 Years a Slave*. It takes place before the American Civil War (1861–1865). Reid played a girl named Emily. Emily is sold and taken away from her mother. It is a very **emotional** movie.

A NEW CITY

Reid moved to Los Angeles, California. But she misses the food in Atlanta.

Reid has played other parts too. Some were guest parts on TV shows. Some were in smaller movies. Reid wants to show all her acting skills. She knows small roles can lead to bigger ones.

Big or small,
Reid is thankful
for every role
that she gets.

15

CHAPTER 3

UP FOR A
Challenge

In 2016 Reid got a part in an American Girl movie. It is based on the American Girl doll named Lea. The movie is called *Lea to the Rescue*. She plays Lea's friend Aki. Aki lives in the Amazon rain forest.

Reid was excited to play the part of Aki. She learned many things for the role.

The Aki scenes for *Lea to the Rescue* were filmed in South Africa. This is because it looks similar to the Amazon.

Reid learned to speak Portuguese to play Aki. She had to speak with an **accent**. Reid liked playing Aki. It was different from her other jobs.

In one role, Reid played the sister of a magician. Reid's character gets kidnapped.

Reid likes making movies more than TV shows. TV shows are often made on a **set**. The actors work at the same set every day. Movies are different. They are often filmed in more than one place. Reid gets to travel to the locations. Sometimes she travels to other countries.

FUTURE
Plans

Reid has lots of plans for the future. She wants to keep acting. Reid wants to try **comedy**. But she does not think she is good at it yet. She knows she needs more practice.

Reid's favorite parts are in **dramas**.

She wants to make action films too.

She would like to be a superhero.

Reid has a good sense of humor. She wants to bring that out in her acting someday.

Ava DuVernay (left) taught Reid about the importance of including many races in her movies.

BIG DREAMS

Reid would also like to be a director someday. She has her own ideas for movies. Reid learned a lot from her director, Ava DuVernay, in *A Wrinkle in Time*. The actors all worked as a team on the movie. Reid saw how teamwork helps make movies successful. She knows it will help make her successful in life too.

Reid wants to inspire people. She wants them to believe in themselves. She does not want **gender** or race to limit them. She wants people to reach their dreams.

FAMILY AND FAITH

Reid's family helps keep her **grounded**. She also has a strong religious faith.

Reid helps others by attending charity events, such as the Children Mending Hearts Gala in June 2018.

GLOSSARY

accent
a way of talking shared by a group of people, such as the people of a country

comedy
a type of entertainment meant to make people laugh

director
the person with artistic control of a movie

dramas
movies or television shows that are serious and realistic

emotional
causing strong emotions or feelings

gender
the behaviors or traits usually associated with either males or females

grounded
to be stable mentally and emotionally

martial arts
a specific form of fighting such as judo, karate, or kung fu

outcast
a person who is cast out by society

relate
to feel connected with something

set
the scenery and props used when shooting a film

TIMELINE

2003: Storm Reid is born.

2012: Reid acts in her first TV movie, *A Cross to Bear*.

2013: Reid lands her first major role in *12 Years a Slave*.

2016: Reid plays Aki in the American Girl movie *Lea to the Rescue*.

2018: Reid stars in the film *A Wrinkle in Time*.

ACTIVITY

ACT IT OUT

Actors often have to show different emotions. Sometimes they must act sad. Sometimes they act excited. Sometimes they act nervous or scared.

You can act out different emotions too. It's fun to guess the emotions with friends or family.

First, think of an emotion you will show. It might be happy, worried, upset, afraid, or relieved. Then, act out the emotion without saying anything. Your audience then guesses what emotion you are trying to show.

FURTHER RESOURCES

Interested in acting? Try some scenes found in this book:

Harbison, Lawrence. *The Best Scenes for Kids Ages 7–15*. Milwaukee, WI: Applause Theare & Cinema Books, 2015.

Want to make your own movie? Find out how:

Stoller, Bryan Michael. *Smartphone Movie Maker*. Somerville, Mass.: Candlewick Press, 2017.

Love the movie *A Wrinkle in Time*? Check out the graphic novel:

Larson, Hope. *A Wrinkle in Time: The Graphic Novel*. New York, NY: Farrar Straus Giroux, 2012.

INDEX

comedy, 22

director, 4, 9, 25
dramas, 23

gender, 26

Lea to the Rescue, 16

martial arts, 11
movies, 5, 7, 9, 13, 14, 16, 21, 25

Portuguese, 19

race, 9, 26

set, 21

teamwork, 25
TV, 14, 21
12 Years a Slave, 13

Wrinkle in Time, A, 7, 25